Pearl of Wisdom:

Buddhist Prayers and Practices

Pearl of Wisdom:
Buddhist Prayers and Practices

Book I

**Foundation for the Preservation of
the Mahayana Tradition**

First published in 1988

For further information, contact:
    Thubten Chodron
    32 Adis Road #01-38
    Singapore 0922

ISBN 981-00-0558-X

Typeset by Lolitho Private Limited
Printed by Ocean Colour Printing Pte Ltd

Contents

Introduction   vii

Heart of Wisdom Sutra   1

Homage to Manjushri   6

Morning Prayers   8

Prayers Before Teachings and Meditation   12

The Foundation of All Good Qualities   26

The Three Principles of the Path   29

Meditation on the Buddha   32

Purification Practices   37
    The Bodhisattvas' Confession of Moral Downfalls   39
    General Confession   44

Dedication Verses   47

Long Life Prayers   54

Offering Food   60

The Eight Mahayana Precepts Ceremony   62

Practicing Dharma in Daily Life   68

The Six Preparatory Practices   76

Meditations on the Gradual Path to Enlightenment   77

Guidelines for the Practice of Refuge   80

A Note on the Translation   83

Notes   84

Introduction

Many people have the question, "Why pray? What are the meaning and purpose of prayer?" Prayers and chanting are not merely moving the mouth; they are moving the mind. They are ways of guiding our thoughts and energy in a certain direction; they are a technique to help us transform our mind. By contemplating the meaning of what we are saying or reading, we make the prayers and practices effective in enriching the quality of our life.

The same prayers and practices are done repeatedly because it takes time for us to transform our mind. Building up good habits of the mind is a gradual process, thus we do the same prayers and practices each day in order to train and familiarize ourselves with a new way of regarding and relating to ourselves and others.

But why say prayers and do practices written by other people? Why not do our own? The great masters have realizations of the gradual path to enlightenment, and the prayers written by them from their own experience show us the correct way to train our mind so that we can develop those same realizations. Of course, having learned well the gradual path to enlightenment, we can still say spontaneous prayers from our heart that express the same meaning in our own words.

Regarding prayer and formal practice as completely distinct from daily life is a deterrent to our progress. A quiet time set aside for prayer and practice helps us concentrate better on transforming our attitudes into beneficial ones. But the testing ground that shows us what qualities are firm within us and which ones still need to be developed more is our daily life with all of its activities. Thus, for the mindful person who is dedicated to developing his/her Buddha potential, the prayer and meditation sessions and the activities of daily life complement each other.

To understand the meaning of each prayer, explanation from a teacher is most helpful. This enables us to understand what qualities the prayers are to designed to develop within us and how to think while doing the recitations. By receiving explanation on the prayers, the meaning of any unfamiliar terms and phrases can also be clarified.

Many thanks are due to those who helped in the preparation of this book. First and foremost, gratitude is due to the Buddha, the lineages of Spiritual Masters, and my own Spiritual Masters, especially His Holiness the Dalai Lama, Tsenzhab Serkong Rinpoche, Lama Yeshe and Zopa Rinpoche. Also, many thanks to all those who translated the prayers and practices, to Thubten Dekyong for checking the translations, and to Thubten Dondrub for his preliminary work and valuable suggestions. All errors are due to my own carelessness.

Thubten Chodron
Singapore, 1988

Heart of Wisdom Sutra

Thus I have heard: at one time, the Blessed One was dwelling in Rajagriha on Massed Vultures Mountain together in one method with a great assembly of monks and a great assembly of bodhisattvas. At that time, the Blessed One was absorbed in the concentration of the countless aspects of phenomena called Profound Illumination.

At that time also Superior Avalokiteshvara, the bodhisattva, the great being, was looking perfectly at the practice of the profound perfection of wisdom, perfectly looking at the emptiness of inherent existence of the five aggregates also.

Then, through the power of Buddha, the Venerable Shariputra said to the Superior Avalokiteshvara, the bodhisattva, the great being, "How should a son of the lineage train who wishes to engage in the practice of the profound perfection of wisdom?"

Thus he spoke, and the Superior Avalokiteshvara, the bodhisattva, the great being, replied to the Venerable Shariputra as follows:

"Shariputra, whatever son or daughter of the lineage wishes to engage in the practice of the profound perfection of wisdom should look perfectly like this: subsequently looking perfectly and correctly at the emptiness of inherent existence of the five aggregates also.

"Form is empty; emptiness is form. Emptiness is not other than form; form also is not other than emptiness. Likewise, feeling, discrimination, compositional factors and consciousness are empty.

"Shariputra, like this all phenomena are merely empty, having no characteristics. They are not produced and do not cease. They have no defilement and no separation from defilement. They have no decrease and no increase.

"Therefore, Shariputra, in emptiness there is no form, no feeling, no discrimination, no compositional factors, no consciousness. There is no eye, no ear, no nose, no tongue, no body, no mind; no form, no sound, no smell, no taste, no tactile object, no phenomenon. There is no eye element and so forth up to no mind element and also up to no element of mental consciousness. There is no ignorance and no exhaustion of ignorance, and so forth up to no ageing and death and no exhaustion of ageing and death. Likewise, there is no suffering, origin, cessation or path; no exalted wisdom, no attainment and also no non-attainment.

"Therefore Shariputra, because there is no attainment, bodhisattvas rely on and abide in the perfection of wisdom; their minds have no obstructions and no fear. Passing utterly beyond perversity, they attain the final state beyond sorrow. Also, all the Buddhas who perfectly reside in the three times, relying upon the perfection of wisdom, become manifest and complete Buddhas in the state of unsurpassed, perfect and complete enlightenment.

"Therefore, the mantra of the perfection of wisdom, the mantra of great knowledge, the unsurpassed mantra, the equal-to-the-unequalled mantra, the mantra that thoroughly pacifies all suffering, since it is not false, should be known as the truth. The mantra of the perfection of wisdom is proclaimed:

tayata gate gate paragate parasamgate bodhi soha

(Gone, gone, gone beyond, gone completely beyond, awakened, so be it!)

"Shariputra, a bodhisattva, a great being, should train in the profound perfection of wisdom like this."

Then the Blessed One arose from that concentration and said to the Superior Avalokiteshvara, the bodhisattva, the great being, that he had spoken well. "Good, good, O son of the lineage. It is like that. Since it is like that, just as you have revealed, the profound perfection of wisdom should be practiced in that way, and the tathagatas will also rejoice."

When the Blessed One had said this, the Venerable Shariputra, the Superior Avalokiteshvara, the bodhisattva, the great being, and that entire assembly of disciples as well as the worldly beings — gods, humans, demi-gods and spirits — were delighted and highly praised what had been spoken by the Blessed One.

(The noble "Heart of the Perfection of Wisdom Sutra" is complete.)

To those from the pure and supreme places who enjoy space (emptiness),
Who possess the five clairvoyances and can magically emanate,
Care for us practitioners, like a mother for her child.
I prostrate to the assembly of dakinis of the three places.

ah ka sama radza sada rasa maraya pey (recite several times),

tayata gate gate paragate parasamgate bodhi soha

By the truth of the existence of the Three Jewels, may all inner and outer hindrances and adversities be overcome! (clap)
May they become non-existent! (clap)
May they be pacified! (clap)
May all negative forces opposed to the Dharma be completely pacified!

May the eighty thousand obstacles be pacified. May we be separated from all adverse conditions and may we obtain conducive circumstances and everything good. May there be auspiciousness, happiness and well-being here, right now!

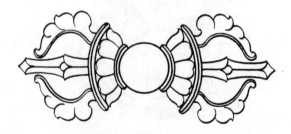

Mañjushrī

Homage to Manjushri, the Buddha of Wisdom

la ma dang gon po je tsun jam pal yang la chak tsal lo
gang gi lo dro drib nyi trin dral nyi tar nam dag rab sal way
ji nye don kun ji zhin zig chir nyi kyi tug kar leg bam dzin
gang dag si pay tson rar ma rig mun tom dug ngal gyi zer way
dro tsog kun la bu chig tar tse yan lag drug chu yang den sung
drug tar cher drog nyon mong nyi long lay kyi chag drog drol
dze ching
ma rig mun sel dug ngal nyu gu ji nye cho dze ral dri nam
do nay dag ching sa chu tar son yon ten lu dzog gyal say tu wo ku
chu trag chu dang chu nyi gyan tra dag loi mun sel jam pal yang
la du
tse den kyo kyi kyen rab wo zer gyi
dag loi ti mug mun pa rab sal nay
ka dang ten cho zhung lug tog pa yi
lo dro pob pay nang wa tsal du sol

Homage to Manjushri, the Buddha of Wisdom

Obeisance to my Guru and Protector, Manjushri,
Who holds to his heart a scriptural text symbolic of his seeing
all things as they are,
Whose intelligence shines forth like the sun, unclouded by
delusions or traces of ignorance,
Who teaches in sixty ways, with the loving compassion of a father
for his only child, all creatures caught in the prison of samsara,
confused in the darkness of their ignorance, overwhelmed by their
suffering.
You, whose dragon-thunder-like proclamation of Dharma arouses
us from the stupor of our delusions and frees us from the iron
chains of our karma;
Who wields the sword of wisdom hewing down suffering wherever
its sprouts appear, clearing away the darkness of ignorance;
You, whose princely body is adorned with the one hundred and
twelve marks of a Buddha,
Who has completed the stages achieving the highest perfection
of a bodhisattva,
Who has been pure from the beginning,
I bow down to you, O Manjushri;
With the brilliance of your wisdom, O compassionate one,
Illuminate the darkness enclosing my mind,
Enlighten my intelligence and wisdom
So that I may gain insight into the Buddha's words and the texts
that explain them.

Morning Prayers

1. Refuge

la ma sang gye la ma cho
day zhin la ma gay dun te
kun gyi je po la ma te
la ma nam la kyab su chi   3x

2. Generating the dedicated heart

dag dang zhan don drup lay du
dag gi jang chub sem kye do   3x

3. Purifying the place

tam chay du ni sa zhi dag
seg ma la sog may pa dang
lag til tar nyam bay dur ye
rang zhin jam por nay gyur chig

4. Offering prayer

lha dang mi yi cho pay dzay
ngo su sham dang yi kyi trul
kun zang cho drin la na may
nam kay kam kun kyab gyur chig

Morning Prayers

1. Refuge

Guru is Buddha, Guru is Dharma. Guru is Sangha also. Guru is the originator of all (goodness and happiness.) To all Gurus, I go for refuge.[1] 3x

2. Generating the dedicated heart

To accomplish my own and others' aims, I generate the heart dedicated to attaining enlightenment for the benefit of all sentient beings. 3x

3. Purifying the place

Everywhere may the ground be pure, free of the roughness of pebbles and so forth. May it be the nature of lapis and as smooth as the palm of one's hand.

4. Offering prayer

May offering substances human and divine, those actual and those which are emanated, unsurpassed Samantabhadra clouds of offerings fill the entire space.

5. Offering dharani (to increase the offerings)

om namo bhagavate bendzay sarwaparma dana tathagataya
arhate samyaksam buddhaya tayata om bendzay bendzay
maha bendzay maha taydza bendzay maha bidya bendzay
maha bodhicitta bendzay maha bodhi mendo pasam kramana
bendzay sarwa karma awarana bisho dana bendzay soha

6. Power of the truth

kon chog sum gyi den pa dang/ sang gye dang jang chub sem
pa tam chay kyi jin gyi lab dang tsog nyi yong su dzog pay
nga tang chen po dang/ cho kyi ying nam par dag ching sam
gyi mi kyab pay tob kyi day zhin nyi du gyur chig

7. Invocation

ma lu sem chen kun gyi gon gyur ching
du te pung chay mi zay jom dzay lha
ngo nam ma lu yang dag kyen gyur pay
chom den kor chay nay dir sheg su sol

8. Prostration mantra

om namo manjushriye namo sushriye namo uttama shriye
soha

9. Homage to the Buddha

la ma ton pa chom dan day/ day zhin sheg pa/ dra chom pa/
yang dag pa dzog pay sang gye/ pal gyal wa shakya tup pa la/
chag tsal ching kyap su chi wo/ cho do/ jin gyi lap tu sol

5. Offering dharani

om namo bhagavate bendzay sarwaparma dana tathagataya arhate samyaksam buddhaya tayata om bendzay bendzay maha bendzay maha taydza bendzay maha bidya bendzay maha bodhicitta bendzay maha bodhi mendo pasam kramana bendzay sarwa karma awarana bisho dana bendazay soha

6. Power of the truth

By the power of the truth of the Three Jewels, the power of the blessings of all the Buddhas and bodhisattvas, the power of the great might of the completed two collections, and the power of the intrinsically pure and inconceivable sphere of reality, may (these offerings) become suchness.

7. Invocation

Protector of all beings without exception, endless subduer of Mara's tribe and forces, deity, perfect knower of all things, Bhagavan and attendants, please come here.

8. Prostration mantra

om namo manjushriye namo sushriye namo uttama shriye soha   3x

9. Homage to the Buddha

To the Guru and Founder, the Endowed Transcendent Destroyer, the One Gone Beyond, the Foe Destroyer, the Completely Perfected, Fully-awakened Being, the Glorious Conqueror, the Subduer from the Shakya Clan, I prostrate, go for refuge and make offerings. Please inspire me.   3x

Prayers Before Teachings and Meditation

1. Refuge

Namo Gurubhya
Namo Buddhaya
Namo Dharmaya
Namo Sanghaya   (Sanskrit)   3x or 7x

la ma la kyab su chi wo
sang gye la kyab su chi wo
cho la kyab su chi wo
gay dun la kyab su chi wo   (Tibetan)

2. Refuge and generating the heart dedicated to attaining enlightenment for the benefit of all sentient beings

sang gye cho dang tsog kyi chog nam la
jang chub bar du dag ni kyab su chi
dag gi *jin sok* gyi pay so nam kyi
drol la pan chir sang gye drub par shog   3x

(before teachings, replace the italic section with:)
cho nyen...

Prayers Before Teachings and Meditation

1. Refuge

I take refuge in the Gurus
I take refuge in the Buddhas
I take refuge in the Dharma
I take refuge in the Sangha   3x or 7x

2. Refuge and generating the heart dedicated to attaining enlightenment for the benefit of all sentient beings

I take refuge until I am enlightened in the Buddhas, the Dharma and the Sangha. By the positive potential I create by *practicing generosity and the other far-reaching attitudes,* may I attain Buddhahood in order to benefit all sentient beings.   3x

(before teachings, replace the italic section with:)
listening to the Dharma...

3. The four immeasurables — short version

sem chen tam che day wa dang day way gyu dang den par
gyur chig
sem chen tam che dug ngel dang dug ngel kyi gyu dang drel
war gyur chig
sem chen tam che dug ngel may pay day wa dang mi drel
war gyur chig
sem chen tam che nye ring chag dang nyi dang drel way
dang nyom la nay par gyur chig

4. The four immeasurables — long version

sem chen tam che nye ring chag dang dang drel way tang
nyom la ne na chi ma rung/ ne par gyur chig/ ne par dag
gi ja wo/ day tar je nu par la ma lha jin gyi lab tu sol

sem chen tam che day wa dang day way gyu dang den na
chi ma rung/ den par gyur chig/ den par dag gi ja wo/ day
tar je nu par la ma lha jin gyi lab tu sol

sem chen tam che dug ngal dang dug ngal gyi gyu dang dral
na chi ma rung/ dral war gyur chig/ dral war dag gi ja wo/
day tar je nu par la ma lha jin gyi lab tu sol

sem chen tam che to ri dang tar pay day wa dam pa dang ma
dral na chi ma rung/ mi dral war gyur chig/ mi dral wa dag
gi ja wo/ day tar je nu par la ma lha jin gyi lab tu sol

5. Special dedicated heart

kye par ma sem chen tam che kyi don du nyur wa nyur war
yang dag par dzog pay sang gye kyi go pang rin po che chi
nay kyang tob par ja/ day chir du lam zab mo la ma lhay
nal jor nyam su lang war gyi wo

3. The four immeasurables — short version

May all sentient beings have happiness and its causes,
May all sentient beings be free of suffering and its causes,
May all sentient beings not be separated from sorrowless bliss,
May all sentient beings abide in equanimity, free of bias, attachment and anger.

4. The four immeasurables — long version

How wonderful it would be if all sentient beings were to abide in equanimity, free of bias, attachment and anger. May they abide in this way. I shall cause them to abide in this way. Guru-deity, please inspire me to be able to do so.

How wonderful it would be if all sentient beings had happiness and its causes. May they have these. I shall cause them to have these. Guru-deity, please inspire me to be able to do so.

How wonderful it would be if all sentient beings were free from suffering and its causes. May they be free. I shall cause them to be free. Guru-deity, please inspire me to be able to do so.

How wonderful it would be if all sentient beings were never parted from upper rebirth and liberation's excellent bliss. May they never be parted. I shall cause them never to be parted. Guru-deity, please inspire me to be able to do so.

5. Special dedicated heart

Especially for the sake of all mother sentient beings, I must quickly and more quickly — in this very life — attain the precious state of complete and perfect Buddhahood. Therefore, I shall practice the profound path of Guru-deity yoga.

6. Seven limb prayer

go sum gu pay go nay chag tsal lo
ngo sham yi trul cho pa ma lu bul
tog may ne sak dig tung tam che shag
kye pa gay wa nam la je yi rang
kor wa ma tong bar du leg zhug nay
dro la cho kyi kor lo kor wa dang
dag zhen gay nam jang chub chen por ngo

7. Long Mandala offering

om vajra bhumi ah hum
wang chen ser gyi sa zhi
om vajra rekhe ah hum
chi chag ri kor yug gi kor way u su
ri gyal po ri rab
shar lu pag po
lho dzam bu ling
nup ba lang cho
jang dra mi nyan

lu dang lu pag
nga yap dang nga yap zhan
yo dan dang lam chog dro
dra mi nyan dang dra mi nyan gyi da

rin po che ri wo
pag sam gyi shing
do joi ba
ma mo pa yi lo tog

6. Seven limb prayer

Reverently I prostrate with my body, speech and mind,
And present clouds of every type of offering, actual and
mentally transformed.
I confess all my negative actions accumulated since begin-
ningless time,
And rejoice in the virtues of all holy and ordinary beings.
Please remain until cyclic existence ends,
And turn the wheel of Dharma for sentient beings.
I dedicate all the virtues of myself and others to the great
enlightenment.

7. Long mandala offering

OM vajra ground AH HUM, mighty golden ground.
OM vajra fence AH HUM, the iron fence around the edge,
In the center is Mount Meru, the king of mountains,
in the east the continent Lupapo
in the south Dzambuling
in the west Balangcho
in the north Draminyan

In the east are the sub-continents Lu and Lupag
in the south Ngayab and Ngayabzhan
in the west Yodan and Lamchog dro
in the north Draminyan and Draminyan Gyida

Here are the precious mountain
the wish-granting tree
the wish-fulfilling cow
the unploughed harvest.

kor lo rin po che
nor bu rin po che
tsun mo rin po che
long po rin po che
lang po rin po che
ta chog rin po che
mag pon rin po che
ter chen poi bum pa

gek ma
treng wa ma
lu ma
gar ma
may tog ma
dug po ma
nang sal ma
dri chap ma

nyi ma
da wa
rin po che dug
chog la nam par gyal way gyal tsan

u su lha dang mi pal jor pun sum tsog pa ma tsang wa may
pa/ tzang zhing yi du wong wa di dag drin chen tza wa dang
gyu par, che pay pal dan la ma dam pa nam dang/ kye par
du yang *la ma lo zang tub wang dor je chang, chen po lha tsog kor
dang che pa nam la* zhing kam bul war gyio/ tug je dro way
don du zhe su sol/ zhe nay kyang dog sog dro wa mar gyur
nam kay ta dang nyam pay sem chen tam che la, tug tze
wa, chen poi go ne jin gyi lab tu sol

Here are the precious wheel
the precious jewel
the precious queen
the precious minister
the precious elephant
the precious horse
the precious general
the great treasure vase.

Here are the goddess of beauty
the goddess of garlands
the goddess of song
the goddess of dance
the goddess of flowers
the goddess of incense
the goddess of light
the goddess of perfume.

Here are the sun
the moon
the precious parasol
the banner of victory in all directions.

In the centre are the most perfect riches of gods and humans, with nothing missing, pure and delightful.

To my glorious, holy and most kind root Guru, the lineage Gurus, and in particular *to the great Lama Tzong Khapa, Buddha who is the King of Sages, Vajradhara, and the entire assembly of deities,* I offer these as a Buddha-field.

Please accept them with compassion, for the sake of migrating beings. Having accepted them, please bestow on me and on mother sentient beings abiding as far as the limits of space your inspiration with loving compassion.

(When requesting teachings, replace the italic section with
the name of the teacher, for example:)
yong dzog ten pay nga dag je tsun Thubten Zopa Rinpoche
pal zang po, zhal nga nay, teg pa chen po, sung cho zab
mo, zhu way yon du...

(After teachings, replace the italic section with:)
yong dzog tan pay nga dag je tsun Thubten Zopa Rinpoche
pal zang po, zhal nga nay, teg pa chen po, sung cho zab
mo, leg par tob pay, ka drin tang rag gi yon du...

8. Short mandala offering

sa zhi po kyi jug shing may tog tram
ri rab ling zhi nyi day gyan pa di
sang gye zhing du mig tay ul war gyi
dro kun nam dag zhing la cho par shog

9. Mandala offering to request teachings

je tsun la ma dam pa kye nam kyi
cho ku ka la kyen tse drin trig nay
ji tar tsam pay dul je zim ma la
zab gye cho ki char pa ab tu sol

10. Inner mandala offering

dag gi chag dang mong sum kye pay yul
dra nyen bar sum lu dang long cho chay
pang pa may par bul gyi leg zhe nay
dug sum rang sar drol war jin gyi lob

(To request teachings, replace the italic section with the name of the teacher, for example:)
to the master of the perfect doctrine, the Venerable Thubten Zopa Rinpoche, glorious and excellent, in order to receive from your mouth the great, profound mahayana teachings...

(After teachings, replace the italic section with:)
to the master of the perfect doctrine, the Venerable Thubten Zopa Rinpoche, glorious and excellent, as an offering to thank you for your kindness as we have received a profound mahayana teaching from you...

8. Short mandala offering

This ground, anointed with perfume, flowers strewn,
Mount Meru, four lands, sun and moon,
Imagined as a Buddha land and offered to you
May all beings enjoy this pure land.

9. Mandala offering to request teachings

Venerable holy Gurus, in the space of your truth body, from billowing clouds of your wisdom and love, let fall the rain of the profound and extensive Dharma in whatever form is suitable for subduing sentient beings.

10. Inner mandala offering

The objects of attachment, aversion and ignorance — friends, enemies and strangers, my body, wealth and enjoyments — I offer these without any sense of loss. Please accept them with pleasure and inspire me and others to be free from the three poisonous attitudes.

Mandala offering after teachings

11. day tar lam zang ton pay shey nyen dang
    tsul zhin drub pay drog nam zhab ten ching
    chi dang nang gi bar du cho pay tsog
    nye war shi war jin gyi lab tu sol

12. je tsun la may ku tse rab ten ching
    nam kar trin lay chog tu gye pa dang
    lo zang ten pa dro may sa sum gi
    dro way mun sel tag tu nay gyur chig

    idam guru ratna mandala kam nirya tayami

Requesting inspiration

13. pal den tsa way la ma rin po che
    dag gi chi wor pay day teng zhug la
    ka drin chen po go nay je zung te
    ku sung tug kyi ngo drub tsal du sol

14. dren pa nyam may ton pa chom den day
    gyal tsab dam pa je tsun mi pam gon
    gyal way lung ten pag pa tog may zhab
    sang gye jang sem sum la sol wa deb

15. jang chub tug la nga nye ser ling pa
    shing ta chen po sol dzin mar may dzay
    lam zang sel dzay ton pa rin po che
    ten pay sog shing sum la sol wa deb

16. ma wa da may dren chog shak yay tog
    gyal way kyen rab kun du jam pay yang
    zab mo don zig pag chog lu drub zhab
    ma way tsug gyen sum la sol wa deb

Mandala offering after teachings

11. May the Spiritual Teachers who lead me on the sacred path and all spiritual friends who practice it have long life. May I pacify completely all outer and inner hindrances — grant such inspiration, I pray.

12. May the lives of the venerable Spiritual Masters be stable, and their white divine actions spread in the ten directions. May the light of Losang's teaching, dispelling the darkness of the beings in the three worlds, always increase.

Idam guru ratna mandala kam nirya tayami

Requesting inspiration

13. Glorious and precious root Guru, sit upon the lotus and moon seat on my crown. Guiding me with your great kindness, bestow upon me the attainments of your body, speech and mind.

14. Buddha, unequalled teacher and guide; Venerable protector Maitreya, his successor; Superior Asanga, prophesied by Buddha; to you three Buddhas and bodhisattvas I make request.

15. Serlingpa, who found the heart of bodhi; Atisha, upholder of this great vehicle; Drom Rinpoche, elucidator of the good path; to you three pillars of the doctrine I make request.

16. Buddha, head of the Shakya clan, the foremost guide, peerless in expounding emptiness; Manjushri, embodiment of the Buddhas' complete wisdom; exalted Nagarjuna, best of the Superiors who see the profound meaning; to you three crowning jewels of clear exposition I make request.

17. ten drel zab mo je shin zig pa yi
  shing ta chen po sol dzin mar may dzay
  lam zang sol dzay ton pa rin po che
  dzam ling gyan gyur nyi la sol wa deb

18. mig may tsay way ter chen chen re zig
  dri may kyen pay wang po jam pel yang
  gang chen kay pay tsug kyen tsong ka pa
  lo zang drag pay zab la sol wa deb

19. lo zang gyal wa kun gyi ye shay ni
  chig du dri may gyal ten dzin pay tso
  rab jam kyil kor gya tso dro du gon
  drin chen la may zab la sol wa deb

20. rab jam sung rab kun la ta way mig
  kal zang tar par dro pay jug ngog chog
  tse way kyo pay tab kay dzay pa yi
  sal dzay shay nyen nam la sol wa deb

17. Atisha, upholder of this great vehicle, who sees the profundity of dependent arising; Drom Rinpoche, elucidator of this good path; to these two ornaments of the world I make request.

18. Avalokiteshvara, great treasure of objectless compassion, Manjushri, master of flawless wisdom, Tzong Khapa, crown jewel of the Snowy Lands' sages, Losang Dragpa, I make request at your holy feet.

19. Losang Yeshe, the transcendental wisdom of the good heart of all the Conquerors, principal holder of the stainless essence of the Conquerors' teachings, protector of the essence of the ocean of profound mandalas, at your holy feet great and kind Master, I make request.

20. The eyes through whom the vast scriptures are seen, supreme doors for the fortunate who would cross over to spiritual freedom, illuminators whose wise means vibrate with compassion, to the entire line of Spiritual Masters I make request.

The Foundation of All Good Qualities
by Lama Tzong Khapa

The kind and venerable Spiritual Master is the foundation of all good qualities. Seeing that dependence on him/her is the root of the path, may I rely on him/her with great respect and continuous effort — inspire me thus!

A human life with leisure is obtained this once. Understanding that it has great value and is hard to find, may I produce unceasingly the mind that takes hold of its essence day and night — inspire me thus!

The fluctuation of our body and life is like a bubble of water; remember death, for we perish so quickly. After death, the effects of black and white karma pursue us as a shadow follows a body.

Finding certainty in this, may I always be careful to abandon even the slightest negative action and to complete the accumulation of virtue — inspire me thus!

There is no satisfaction in enjoying worldly pleasures. They are the door to all misery. Having realized that the fault of samsaric perfections is that they cannot be trusted, may I be strongly intent on the bliss of liberation — inspire me thus!

That pure thought (to attain liberation) produces great conscientiousness, mindfulness and awareness. May I make the essential practice keeping the vows of individual liberation,[2] the root of the doctrine — inspire me thus!

Having seen that all beings, my kind mothers, have fallen like myself into the ocean of cyclic existence, may I train in the supreme heart dedicated to enlightenment, assuming the obligation to free all migrating beings — inspire me thus!

Generating the dedicated heart alone, without cultivation of the three moral practices,[3] does not lead to enlightenment. Having realized this, may I practice with intense effort the vows of the Conquerors and their spiritual children — inspire me thus!

By quieting distraction to false objects, and analyzing the meaning of reality,[4] may I quickly generate within my mind stream the path uniting calm abiding and special insight[5] — inspire me thus!

When, trained in the common path,[6] I am a suitable vessel, let me enter with ease the great gateway of the fortunate ones, the Vajrayana,[7] the highest of all vehicles — inspire me thus!

The basis of achieving the two powerful attainments is the pure vows and commitments that I have pledged. Having found true understanding of this, may I keep them even at the cost of my life — inspire me thus!

Having realized the significance of the two stages,[8] which are the essence of the tantric path, may I steadfastly practice without laziness the four sessions of yoga, and realize what the holy beings have taught — inspire me thus!

May the Spiritual Teachers who lead me on the sacred path and all spiritual friends who practice it have long life. May I quickly and completely pacify all outer and inner hindrances — grant such inspiration, I pray!

In all my rebirths may I never be separated from perfect Spiritual Masters, and enjoy the magnificent Dharma. Completing all qualities of the stages and paths, may I quickly achieve the stage of Vajradhara.[9]

Je Tsongkhapa

The Three Principles of the Path
by Lama Tzong Khapa

I bow down to the venerable Spiritual Masters.

I will explain, as well as I am able, the essence of all the teachings of the Conqueror, the path praised by the Conquerors and their spiritual children, the entrance for the fortunate ones who desire liberation.

Listen with clear minds, you fortunate ones who direct your minds to the path pleasing to the Buddha and strive to make good use of leisure and opportunity without being attached to the joys of cyclic existence.

For you embodied beings bound by the craving for existence, without the pure determination to be free (renunciation) from the ocean of existence, there is no way for you to pacify the attractions to its pleasurable effects. Thus, from the outset seek to generate the determination to be free.

By contemplating the leisure and endowments so difficult to find and the fleeting nature of your life, reverse the clinging to this life. By repeatedly contemplating the infallible effects of karma and the miseries of cyclic existence, reverse the clinging to future lives.

By contemplating in this way, do not generate even for an instant the wish for the pleasures of cyclic existence. When you have, day and night unceasingly, the mind aspiring for liberation, then you have generated the determination to be free.

However, if your determination to be free is not sustained by the pure dedicated heart (bodhicitta), it does not become the cause for the perfect bliss of unsurpassed enlightenment. Therefore, the intelligent generate the supreme thought of enlightenment.

Swept by the current of the four powerful rivers, tied by the strong bonds of karma which are so hard to undo, caught in the iron net of self-grasping egoism, completely enveloped by the darkness of ignorance,

Born and reborn in boundless cyclic existence, unceasingly tormented by the three miseries — by thinking of all mother sentient beings in this condition, generate the supreme altruistic aspiration.

Even if you meditate upon the determination to be free and the mind of enlightenment, without the wisdom realizing the final nature (how things actually exist), you cannot cut the root of cyclic existence. Therefore, strive for the means to realize dependent arising.

One who sees the infallible cause and effect of all phenomena in cyclic existence and beyond and destroys all false perceptions (of their inherent existence) has entered the path which pleases the Buddha.

Appearances are infallible dependent arisings; emptiness is free of assertions (of inherent existence or non-existence). As long as these two understandings are seen as separate, one has not yet realized the intent of the Buddha.

When these two realizations are simultaneous and concurrent, from the mere sight of infallible dependent arising comes definite knowledge which completely destroys all modes of mental grasping. At that time, the analysis of the profound view is complete.

In addition, appearances clear away the extreme of (inherent) existence; emptiness clears away the extreme of non-existence. When you understand the arising of cause and effect from the viewpoint of emptiness, you are not captivated by either of the extreme views.

In this way, when you have realized the exact points of the three principal aspects of the path, by depending on solitude, generate the power of joyous effort and quickly accomplish the final goal, my child!

Meditation on the Buddha

Taking refuge and generating the altruistic heart dedicated to attaining enlightenment for the benefit of all sentient beings

I take refuge until I am enlightened in the Buddhas, the Dharma and the Sangha. Through the positive potential I create by practicing generosity and the other far-reaching attitudes, may I attain Buddhahood in order to benefit all sentient beings.   3x

In order to help all sentient beings and lead them to the perfect peace and happiness of enlightenment, I must attain enlightenment. For this purpose, I shall meditate on Guru Shakyamuni Buddha.

Visualization

Every aspect of the following visualization is made of light — transparent, intangible and radiant. At the level of your forehead, about five or six feet in front of you, visualize a large golden throne adorned with jewels and supported at each corner by a pair of snow lions. On the throne is an open lotus, and on that two discs — the moon and the sun.[10]

Seated upon this is the Buddha, one who has purified all defilements and attained all perfect realizations. He is the embodiment of all enlightened beings. His body is made of golden light and he wears the saffron robes of a monk. He is seated in the vajra posture. The palm of his right hand rests on his right knee, the fingers touching the moon cushion to symbolize his great control. His left hand rests in his lap in the meditation pose, holding a bowl filled with nectar, which is medicine for curing our disturbing attitudes and other hindrances.[11] Feel that this is the real Buddha in front of you.

Buddha's face is very beautiful; his smiling, compassionate gaze is directed towards you and simultaneously encompasses all sentient beings. He is free of all judgemental, critical thoughts and accepts you just as you are. His eyes are long, narrow and very peaceful. His lips are red and his earlobes long. His hair is blue-black and each hair is individually curled to the right. Each feature of his holy body represents an aspect of his omniscient mind.[12]

Rays of light emanate from each pore of Buddha's body and reach every corner of the universe. These rays are composed of countless miniature Buddhas, some going out to help sentient beings, others dissolving back into the Buddha's body after having finished their work.

Around you are seated all sentient beings in human form — friends, strangers and enemies. You are all facing the Buddha together.

Purification

Feel the living presence of the Buddha and take refuge in him, recalling his perfect qualities and his willingness and ability to help you. Make a request from your heart to receive his inspiration and blessings to help you and others become free from all of your negative energy, disturbing attitudes, misconceptions and problems. Request to receive all the realizations of the path to enlightenment so that you may be peaceful and happy and be able to make your life beneficial for others. Recite the following, in Tibetan or English, three times:

la ma ton pa chom dan de / de zhin sheg pa / dra chom pa / yang dag pa dzog pay sang gye / pal gyal wa shakya tup pa la / chag tsal ching kyap su chi wo / cho do / jin gyi lap tu sol

To the Guru and Founder, the Endowed Transcendent Destroyer, the One Gone Beyond, the Foe Destroyer, the Completely Perfected, Fully-awakened Being, the Glorious Conqueror, the Subduer from the Shakya Clan, I prostrate, go for refuge and make offerings. Please bestow upon me your inspiration.

Your request is accepted. A stream of purifying white light, which is the nature of the enlightened mind of wisdom and compassion, flows from the Buddha's heart and enters your body through the crown of your head. The light also flows into all the sentient beings, whom you have visualized sitting around you. Just as the darkness in a room is instantly dispelled the moment a light is switched on, so too is the darkness of your negative energy dispelled as soon as the radiant white light enters you. Continue with the visualization while reciting the Buddha's mantra as many times as you wish:

tayata om muni muni maha muniye soha

Feel that the negative energy, problems and subtle obscurations of yourself and others have been completely purified. Your body is filled with light and is very blissful. Concentrate on this for a while.

Receiving inspiration and blessings

Visualize that a stream of golden light, the essence of which is the excellent qualities of the Buddha's body, speech and mind,[13] descends from the Buddha's heart and flows into you and into all the sentient beings around you through the crown of your head. These infinite good qualities permeate every part of you. Concentrate on this blissful experience of receiving the blessings and inspiration of the Buddha while reciting:

tayata om muni muni maha muniye soha

Feel that you have received the infinite excellent qualities of the Buddha. You have unbiased love and compassion for all beings, just as the Buddha does. Feel that you have actualized the six far-reaching attitudes: generosity, morality, patience, joyous effort, concentration and wisdom. It is the same for all the sentient beings around you. Feel blissful and satisfied. Concentrate on this for some time.

Absorption

Make a determined aspiration to live your life according to the loving and compassionate thought to become a Buddha for the benefit of all sentient beings. Think that Guru Shakyamuni Buddha is extremely pleased with your noble aspiration, and will guide you so that you can actualize it.

Visualize that the throne absorbs into the lotus, and the lotus into the moon and sun discs. They, in turn, absorb into the Buddha, who now comes above your head, facing the same way as you do. He melts into light and dissolves into you, thus blessing, inspiring and transforming your mind. Feel that not even the slightest bit of selfishness remains and that your mind has become the loving, compassionate thought aspiring to attain enlightenment only for the benefit of others.

Reappearance

At your heart center appears a small Buddha, made of light.[14] Be mindful of the Buddha at your heart as you do all the daily activities of your life.

Dedication

Due to this merit may I soon
Attain the enlightened state of Guru-Buddha,
That I may be able to liberate
All sentient beings from their sufferings.

May the precious bodhi mind
Not yet born arise and grow.
May that born have no decline,
But increase forever more.

Purification Practices

There are a variety of purification practices, "The Bodhisattva's Confession of Moral Downfalls" being one of the most popular. We all have done actions that we now feel badly about doing, and we have aspects of ourselves that we do not like and wish to change. Purification practices are excellent means to remove emotional burdens such as guilt, as well as to pacify the obstacles to our happiness and self-improvement created by the imprints of our destructive actions. Guilt over past actions is useless, only leaving us feeling helpless and hopeless. On the other hand, acting to purify the negative imprints and disturbing attitudes is very productive. It helps us to change our bad habits, and subdues obstacles to long life and success in our spiritual practice.

A complete purification practice consists of four opponent powers:

1. The power of regret for having done the negative action.

2. The power of reliance: taking refuge, which corrects our relationship with holy objects, and generating the altruistic dedicated heart, which corrects our relationship with other sentient beings.

3. The power of the remedial action, e.g. prostration, offering, reciting the names of the Buddha, reading or contemplating the Dharma, etc.

4. The power of the promise not to repeat the action.

These four opponent powers are found in "The Bodhisattva's Confession of Moral Downfalls," the Vajrasattva meditation, and other practices.

There are several visualizations of the thirty-five Buddhas. The easiest is to visualize Shakyamuni Buddha, golden in color, with thirty-four light rays coming from his heart. These light rays form five rows and upon each ray is seated a Buddha. The Buddhas in each row resemble one of the five Dhyani Buddhas.

In the first row, are the next six Buddhas mentioned in the prayer. They resemble Akshobya Buddha, blue, the left hand in his lap in the gesture of meditative equipoise, the right hand in the earth-touching gesture (on the right knee, palm down). However, the One Thus Gone, the King with Power over the Nagas, looks slightly different: he has a blue body, a white face, and his hands are folded together at his heart.

In the second row, the next seven Buddhas resemble Vairocana Buddha, white, with both hands at the heart, the index fingers extended.

In the third row, the next seven Buddhas resemble Ratnasambhava Buddha, yellow. His left hand is in meditative equipoise, and his right hand is in the gesture of giving (on the right knee, palm outwards).

In the fourth row, the next seven Buddhas resemble Amitabha Buddha, red, with both hands in meditative equipoise on his lap.

In the fifth row, the next seven Buddhas resemble Amogasiddhi Buddha, green, the left hand is in meditative equipoise and the right hand, bent at the elbow, the palm facing outwards.

Visualize that you are surrounded by all sentient beings in human form and that you are leading them in prostrating to the Buddhas. While prostrating, imagine much light coming from the Buddhas and flowing into you and into all the sentient beings around you. This light purifies all imprints of negative actions and all disturbing attitudes.

The Bodhisattvas's Confession of Moral Downfalls
Prostrations to the Thirty-Five Buddhas

To increase the benefit of each prostration, first prostrate three times while reciting:

om namo manjushriye namo sushriye namo uttama shriye soha.

Continue to prostrate while reciting the names of the Buddhas and the confession prayer.

I, (say your name) throughout all times, take refuge in the Gurus; I take refuge in the Buddhas; I take refuge in the Dharma; I take refuge in the Sangha.

To the Founder, the Transcendent Destroyer, the One Thus Gone,[15] the Foe Destroyer, the Fully Enlightened One, the Glorious Conqueror from the Shakyas I bow down.

To the One Thus Gone, the Great Destroyer, Destroying with Vajra Essence I bow down.

To the One Thus Gone, the Jewel Radiating Light I bow down.

To the One Thus Gone, the King with Power over the Nagas I bow down.

To the One Thus Gone, the Leader of the Warriors I bow down.

To the One Thus Gone, the Glorious Blissful One I bow down.

To the One Thus Gone, the Jewel Fire I bow down.

To the One Thus Gone, the Jewel Moonlight I bow down.
To the One Thus Gone, Whose Pure Vision Brings Accomplish-
    ments I bow down.
To the One Thus Gone, the Jewel Moon I bow down.
To the One Thus Gone, the Stainless one I bow down.
To the One Thus Gone, the Glorious Giver I bow down.
To the One Thus Gone, the Pure One I bow down.
To the One Thus Gone, the Bestower of Purity I bow down.

To the One Thus Gone, the Celestial Waters I bow down.
To the One Thus Gone, the Deity of the Celestial Waters
    I bow down.
To the One Thus Gone, the Glorious Good I bow down.
To the One Thus Gone, the Glorious Sandalwood I bow down.
To the One Thus Gone, the One of Unlimited Splendor
    I bow down.
To the One Thus Gone, the Glorious Light I bow down.
To the One Thus Gone, the Glorious One without Sorrow
    I bow down.

To the One Thus Gone, the Son of the Desireless One
    I bow down.
To the One Thus Gone, the Glorious Flower I bow down.
To the One Thus Gone, Who Understands Reality
    Enjoying the Radiant Light of Purity I bow down.
To the One Thus Gone, Who Understands Reality
    Enjoying the Radiant Light of the Lotus I bow down.
To the One Thus Gone, the Glorious Gem I bow down.
To the One Thus Gone, the Glorious One who is Mindful
    I bow down.
To the One Thus Gone, the Glorious One Whose Name is
    Extremely Renowned, I bow down.

To the One Thus Gone, the King Holding the Banner of
Victory over the Senses I bow down.

To the One Thus Gone, the Glorious One Who Subdues
Everything Completely I bow down.

To the One Thus Gone, the Victorious One in All Battles
I bow down.

To the One Thus Gone, the Glorious One Gone to Perfect
Self-control I bow down.

To the One Thus Gone, the Glorious One Who Enhances and
Illuminates Completely I bow down.

To the One Thus Gone, the Jewel Lotus Who Subdues All
I bow down.

To the One Thus Gone, the Foe Destroyer, the Fully Enlightened
One, the King with Power over Mount Meru, Always
Remaining in the Jewel and the Lotus I bow down.

All you thirty-five Buddhas, and all the others, those thus gone,
foe destroyers, fully enlightened ones and transcendent destroyers
who are existing, sustaining and living throughout the ten
directions of sentient beings' worlds — all you Buddhas, please
give me your attention.

In this life, and throughout beginningless lives in all the realms
of samsara, I have created, caused others to create, and rejoiced
at the creation of negative karmas such as misusing offerings to
holy objects, misusing offerings to the Sangha, stealing the posses-
sions of the Sangha of the ten directions; I have caused others
to create these negative actions and rejoiced at their creation.

I have created the five heinous actions,[16] caused others to create
them and rejoiced at their creation. I have committed the ten
non-virtuous actions,[17] involved others in them, and rejoiced in
their involvement.

Being obscured by all this karma, I have created the cause for myself and other sentient beings to be reborn in the hells, as animals, as hungry ghosts, in irreligious places, amongst barbarians, as long-lived gods, with imperfect senses, holding wrong views, and being displeased with the presence of a Buddha.

Now before these Buddhas, transcendent destroyers who have become transcendental wisdom, who have become the compassionate eye, who have become witnesses, who have become valid and see with their omniscient minds, I am confessing and accepting all these actions as negative. I will not conceal or hide them, and from now on, I will refrain from committing these negative actions.

Buddhas and transcendent destroyers, please give me your attention: in this life and throughout beginningless lives in all the realms of samsara, whatever root of virtue I have created through even the smallest acts of charity such as giving one mouthful of food to a being born as an animal, whatever root of virtue I have created by keeping pure morality, whatever root of virtue I have created by abiding in pure conduct, whatever root of virtue I have created by fully ripening sentient beings' minds, whatever root of virtue I have created by generating bodhicitta: whatever root of virtue I have created of the highest transcendental wisdom.

Bringing together all these merits of both myself and others, I now dedicate them to the highest of which there is no higher, to that even above the highest, to the highest of the high, to the higher of the high. Thus I dedicate them completely to the highest, fully accomplished enlightenment.

Just as the Buddhas and transcendent destroyers of the past have dedicated, just as the Buddhas and transcendent destroyers of the future will dedicate, and just as the Buddhas and transcendent destroyers of the present are dedicating, in the same way I make this dedication.

I confess all my negative actions separately and rejoice in all merits. I implore all the Buddhas to grant my request that I may realize the ultimate, sublime, highest transcendental wisdom.

To the sublime kings of the human beings living now, to those of the past, and to those who have yet to appear, to all those whose knowledge is as vast as an infinite ocean, I go for refuge.

General Confession

So be it!

O Spiritual Masters, great Vajra Holders, and all the Buddhas and bodhisattvas who abide in the ten directions, as well as all the venerable Sangha, please pay attention to me.

I, who am named _____, circling in cyclic existence since beginningless time until the present, overpowered by mental distortions such as attachment, aversion and ignorance, have created the ten negative actions by means of body, speech and mind. I have engaged in the five heinous actions and the five parallel heinous actions.[18] I have transgressed the vows of individual liberation,[19] contradicted the trainings of a bodhisattva,[20] broken the tantric commitments.[21] I have been disrespectful to my kind parents, Spiritual Masters, spiritual friends, and those following the pure paths. I have committed actions harmful to the Three Jewels, avoided the holy Dharma, stolen from the Sangha, and harmed living beings. These and many other destructive actions I have done, have caused others to do, and have rejoiced in others' doing. In short, I have created many obstacles to my own higher rebirth and liberation, and have planted countless seeds for further wanderings in cyclic existence and miserable states of being.

Now in the presence of the Spiritual Masters, the great Vajra Holders, all the Buddhas and bodhisattvas who abide in the ten directions, and the venerable Sangha, I confess all of these negative actions, I will not conceal them and I accept them as negative. I promise to refrain from doing these actions again in the future. By confessing and acknowledging them, I will attain and abide in happiness, while by not confessing and acknowledging them, true happiness will not come.

Dedication Verses

1. gay wa di yi nyur du dag
   la ma sang gye drub gyur nay
   dro wa chig kyang ma lu pa
   kye kyi sa la go par shog

2. jang chub sem chog rin po che
   ma kye pa nam kye gyur chig
   kye pa nyam pa may pa yang
   gong nay gong du pel war shog

3. kye wa kun tu yang dag la ma dang
   dral may cho kyi pal la long cho ching
   sa dang lam gyi yon ten rab dzog nay
   dor je chang gi go pang nyur tob shog

4. tong ngam to sam je su teng kyang rung
   reg kam tam du jo pu tsam gya jang
   day yi mo la dung wa kun shi nay
   nam par kun du day dang den gyur chig

5. ton pa la na may pay ten pa dang
   jal wa di dra la may drin yin pay
   gay wa di yang dro wa ma lu pa
   shay nyen dam pa dzin pay gyu ru ngo

Dedication Verses

Dedication of positive potential (merit) is very important, as it prevents one's positive potential from being destroyed by anger or wrong views. Dedicate the positive potential created by oneself and others in the past, present and future in the following ways:

1. Due to this merit may I soon
   Attain the enlightened state of Guru-Buddha,
   That I may be able to liberate
   All sentient beings from their sufferings.

2. May the precious bodhi mind
   Not yet born arise and grow.
   May that born have no decline,
   But increase forever more.

3. In all my rebirths may I never be separated from perfect Spiritual Masters and enjoy the magnificent Dharma. Completing all qualities of the stages and paths, may I quickly achieve the state of Vajradhara.

4. May anyone who merely sees, hears, remembers, touches or talks to me be freed in that very instant from all sufferings and abide in happiness forever.

5. It is only from the kindness of my Spiritual Masters that I have met the peerless teachings of the Buddha. Thus, I dedicate all positive potential so that all migrating beings may be guided in the future by kind and holy Spiritual Masters.

6. pen dze day yi ten pang si pay tar
   ngen tog lung gi nam par mi yo shing
   ten pay ngang tsul shay ne ton pa la
   yi chay nye pay tar tu kang war shog

7. den pa chog day ka wa pak may kyi
   nen ten nying po dze ne drub pa di
   tab gang shig gi pel war gyur nyam pay
   nam par cho pay nyin tsen da war shog

8. pa ma sem chen tam che day dang den gyur chig
   ngen dro tam cho tak tu tong war tang
   jang chub sem pa kang na su shug pa
   day dag kun gyi mon lam drub gyur chig

9. dro way dug ngel kang che rung
   day kun dag la min gyur chig
   dag gyi day gay chi sag pa
   day kun dag la min gyur chig

10. pal den la may ku tze ten pa dang
    ka nyam yong la day kyi jung wa dang
    dag zhan ma lu tsog sag drib jang nay
    nyur du sang gye tob par jin gyi lob

11. pal den la may nam par tar pa la
    kay chig tsam yang lok ta mi kye shing
    chi dze leg par tong way mo go kyi
    la may jin lab sem la jug par shog

12. pal den la ma kyo ku chi dra dang
    kor dang ku tse tsay dang zhing kam sog
    kyo kyi tsen chog zang po chi dra war
    day dra ko nar dag sog gyur war shog

6. Until cyclic existence ends, may the beneficial teachings not be blown away by the wind of superstitions. May the entire world be filled with people who have understood and found firm faith in the true teachings.

7. Day and night, may I pass the time thinking and examining by what means these teachings can spread in the minds of myself and others.

8. May sentient beings, who have all been my mother and father, be completely happy, and may the lower realms be forever empty. May all the prayers of bodhisattvas, in whatever places they live, be immediately fulfilled.

9. May I experience whatever sufferings sentient beings have, and they experience whatever happiness and virtue I have.

10. May the glorious Spiritual Masters live long, and may all beings throughout limitless space have happiness. By purifying our defilements and accumulating positive potential, may I and all others be blessed (inspired) to attain Buddhahood quickly.

11. May I never develop for even a moment wrong views towards the deeds of my glorious Spiritual Masters. By seeing whatever actions they do as pure with respect and devotion, may the Spiritual Masters' inspiration flow into my mind.

12. In whatever way you appear, O glorious Guru, whatever your retinue, lifespan and pureland, whatever your name most noble and holy, may I and all others attain only these.

13. jam pel pa wo ji tar kyen pa dang
    kun tu zang po de yang de shin tay
    de dag kun gyi je su dag lob chi
    gay wa di dag tam chay rab tu ngo

14. du sum sheg pay gyal wa tam chay kyi
    ngo wa gang la chog tu ngag pa de
    da gyi gay way tsa wa di kun kyang
    sang po cho chir rab tu ngo war gyi

15. tse rab kun tu gyal wa tsong kha pay
    teg chog shay nyen ngo su dzay pay tu
    gyal way ngag pay lam zang de nyi lay
    kay chig tsam yang dog par ma gyur chig

16. tsul trim tsang shing mang du to pa dang
    jang sem jong shing ta cho tsang wa sog
    lo sang gyal wa nyi pay ten pa la
    so lay may pay nam tar kyong war shog

Lam Rim Dedication Prayer

der ni ring du bay lay tsog nyi ni
ka tar yang pa gang shig sag pa de
lo mig ma rig gi dong dro wa nam
nam dren gyal way wong por dag gyur chig

der ma son pay tse rab kun tu yang
jam pel yang kyi tze way je zung nay
ten pay rim pa kun tsang lam gyi chog
nye nay drub pay gyal nam nye je shog

rang gi ji zhin tog pay lam gyi nay
shug drag tze way drang pay tab kay kyi
dro way yi kyi mun pa sel jay nay
gyal way ten pa yun ring dzin gyur chig

13. In order to follow the excellent examples set by the wisdom of the bodhisattva Manjushri and the always sublime Samantabhadra, I dedicate all virtues to their peerless ideals.

14. All Conquerors passed into the three times have praised as supreme this peerless dedication. Therefore, I also surrender all roots of my activities to the sublime goals of a bodhisattva.

15. In all our lives, through the Victorious One, Lama Tzong Khapa acting as the actual Mahayana Spiritual Master, may I never turn aside for even an instant from the excellent path praised by the Victorious Ones.

16. May I and others be able to live in pure moral conduct, train our minds in bodhicitta, and develop pure view and conduct. In this way, may we complete our lives without corrupting the pure wisdom of Lama Tzong Khapa, (who is like) the second Buddha.

Dedication Prayer of the Gradual Path to Enlightenment

From my two collections, vast as space, that I have amassed from working with effort at this practice for a great length of time, may I become the chief leading Buddha for all those whose mind's wisdom eye is blinded by ignorance.

Even if I do not reach this state, may I be held in your loving-compassion for all my lives, Manjushri. May I find the best of complete graded paths of the teachings, and may I please all the Buddhas by practicing well.

Using skilful means drawn by the strong force of compassion, may I clear the darkness from the minds of all beings with the points of the path as I have discerned them; may I uphold Buddha's teachings for a very long time.

ten pa rin chen chog gi ma kyab pam
kyab kyang nyam par gyur pay chog der ni
nying je chen po yi rab kyo pa yi
pen de ter de sel war je par shog

say chay gyal way may jung trin lay lay
leg drub jang chub lam gyi rim pay kyang
tar do nam kyi yi la pel ter zhing
gyal way dzay pa ring du kyong gyur chig

lam zang drub pay tun kyen drub je ching
gyal kyen sel je mi dang mi min kun
tse rab kun tu gyal way ngag pa yi
nam dag lam dang drel war ma gyur chig

gang tse teg pa chog la cho cho chu
tsul zhin drub la tzon pa de yi tse
tu den nam kyi tag tu drog je ching
tra shi gya tso chog kun kyab gyur chig

Request to Lama Tzong Khapa

mig may tse way ter chen chen re zig
dri may kyen pay wang po jam pel yang
gang chen kay pay tsug gyan tsog kha pa
lo zang drag pay shab la sol wa deb

With my heart going out with great compassion in whatever directions the most precious teachings have not yet spread, or once spread have declined, may I expose this treasure of happiness and aid.

May the minds of those who wish for liberation be granted bounteous peace, and the Buddhas' deeds be nourished for a long time by this gradual path to enlightenment completed due to the wondrous virtuous conduct of the Buddhas and their spiritual children.

May all human and non-human beings who eliminate adversity and make things conducive for practicing the excellent paths never be parted in any of their lives from the purest path praised by the Buddhas.

Whenever someone makes effort to act in accordance with the ten-fold Mahayana virtuous practices, may he/she always be assisted by the mighty ones; and may oceans of prosperity spread everywhere.

Request to Lama Tzong Khapa

Avalokiteshvara, great treasure of objectless compassion,
Manjushri, master of flawless wisdom,
Tzong Khapa, crown jewel of the Snowy Lands' sages
Lobsang Drakpa, I make request at your holy feet.   3x

Long Life Prayers

Long Life Prayer for His Holiness the Dalai Lama

gang ri ra way kor way zhing kam dir
pan dang de wa ma lu jung way nay
chen re sig wang ten zin gya tso yi
zhap pay si te bar du ten gyur chig

Long Life Prayer for Venerable Zopa Rinpoche

tse ta yey sok tsa sum gyal wa yi
ye she do gur gyur way trin pung lay
nor bu dru char pen de pal jin pay
gay lek shay pay nang wa kyab dal tsol

tup ten dze pay lap sum ngur mig dzin
rap jam gyu de gya tso nal jor la
tson pay kay tup zo pay gong go nay
du shi yul lay nam gyal zhab tan sol

kal zang dul ja tar pay lam zang la
tri wa tap kay dze pay may jung wa
pal chen dam pay nam tar je dro way
gay tsan ser gyi nyi ma tag char shog

tsul trim tsang zhing mang du to pa shog
jang sem jong la ta cho tsang wa dang
lo zang gyal wa nyi pay dan pa la
say lay may pay nam tar kyong war shog

Long Life Prayers

Long Life Prayer for His Holiness the Dalai Lama

In the snowy mountain paradise
You're the source of good and happiness,
Powerful Tenzin Gyatso Chenresig,
May you stay until samsara ends.

Long Life Prayer for Venerable Zopa Rinpoche

From the clouds of the wisdom of Amitayus and others, three principal Conquerors, transformed into all we desire, grant all-pervading light of goodness and fortune, giving abundant well-being in jewel-like rain!

You who wear the three trainings' red robes that beautify the sage's teachings; in armour that bears the hardships of striving in tantra's infinite ocean-like yogas, one victorious over the four maras — please live long!

Your marvellous skilful deeds conducting fortunate disciples upon the good path to liberation; propitious golden sun who follows the pattern of all the holy beings, shine for ever!

Pure in morality, learned and so forth, of pure view and conduct in the bodhisattva's training, not diluting the teaching of Losang, the second Conqueror — let us cherish this saintly life!

kye wa kun tu yang dag la ma dang
dral may cho kyi pal la long cho ching
sa dang lam gyi yon ten rab dzog nay
dor je chang gi go pang nyur tob shog

may jung say chay gyal way jin lop dang
ten drel lu wa may pay den pa dang
dag gi lhag sam dag pay tu tup kyi
mon pay don kun de lag nyur drup shog

Long Life Prayer for Lama Osel Rinpoche

HRI

tsan pay sel dzong gang ri dang trog ma
tong na yi trog to na yi dung sel
dran na du min jig pa kun lay kyob
tse jin yi zhin kor lo shi pa tsol

tub ten nying chu gan den lug zang gi
leg shay o kyi na tsog dul ja yi
mo kam tun par sel dze cho kyi je
je tsun la ma chog la sol wa deb

lag par nub chog sa tay dro wa la
gyal wa kun lay lag pay drin chen je
lar yang sam zhin chog tay rig ru su
jon la ka drin dran pay kyo shab sol

In all our rebirths may we never be separated from perfect Gurus and enjoy the magnificent Dharma. Completing all qualities of the stages and paths, may we quickly achieve the state of Vajradhara.

By the power inspiration of the marvellous Conquerors and their spiritual children, by the power of the non-deceptive truth of dependent arising, and by the power of our pure, special intention, may all wished-for aims be accomplished quickly and easily!

Long Life Prayer for Lama Osel Rinpoche

HRI

Enchanting Mother — like a brilliant snow mountain — the shining consummation of signs and marks, who when seen captivates minds, who when heard soothes the sorrows of heart, who when recalled protects from all fears of the untimely, O giver of life, O wish-granting wheel, grant that all may be auspicious.

Lord of Dharma, who in accordance with the various dispositions of those to be subdued makes clear, in the light of your well-spoken advice, the sacred Ganden Tradition — essence of Buddha's Teachings, O foremost and holy Lama, to you who are supreme we make this prayer of supplication.

Venerable one, to you whose kindness exceeds that of all the Conquerors, for those wanderers in far-off places, especially the West; mindful of your loving-concern for us, in intentionally descending again into a family of a far-distant land, we make this request, O Lama please live long.

dri may do ngag yong la ke pay gon
yong dzin shay nyen dam pa tsug ten tog
ke tsun zang po min drol lam zang la
tri way tab ke chen po kyo shab sol

ten pay nying po dul way cho tsul la
bag yo trim tsor zung dang zhan du yang
rab jam do gyu gya tso pa ta ru
son te yong dzog dag por zhab ten shog

tse rab du mar lay mon zang po tu
drin chan la ma chog dang mi dral war
nye shin je su dzin pay bu lob nam
sung gi du tsir ro yi tag tsim shog

gang gi ka drin nying nay dran zhin du
gang nu to dang sam gom la tson pay
ten gyi don chen kal zang nyur tob la
la ma yi dam sung may jin drog dzo

Complete holder, scholar and protector of stainless sutra and tantra, holy spiritual friend, foundation of our unwavering constant devotion, profoundly skilled in methods leading us along the fortunate path of liberation — unfolding within us all that is moral, warm and wise, O Lama please live long.

Master of the entire doctrine — having crossed to the furthermost shore of the vast ocean of sutra and tantra, observing ethics as the foundation of practice, and as the heart of the teaching, conscientiously following Vinaya, O Lama please live long.

By the power of our pure prayer and karma, without our ever being separated from our supremely kind Lama, may we be joyfully guided as your children-disciples throughout infinite lives, and by the sweet nectar taste of your holy speech, may we be forever satisfied.

O Spiritual Masters, deities and protectors, bless us and help us so that we may accomplish the ultimate meaning of life in our striving to listen, reflect and meditate as much as we are able, so that we may quickly usher in a golden age, and so that all the while, we may always remember from the depths of our hearts, the loving-kindness of our precious Lama.

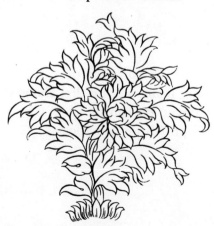

Offering Food

Any or a combination of the following verses may be used to offer one's food before eating.

la ma sang gye la ma cho
de zhin la ma gay dun tay
kun gyi je po la ma tay
la ma nam la cho pa bul

pun tsog gay leg je way drun pay ku
ta ye dron way ray wa kong way sung
ma lu shay ja ji zhin zig pay tug
sha kyay tso wo de la cho pa bul

ton pa la may sang gye rin po che
cho pa la may dam cho rin po che
dren pa la may gay dun rin po che
kyab nay kun du kyo la cho pa bul

dag sog kor chay tse rab tam chay du
kon chog sum dang nam yang mi drel zhing
kon chog sum po gyun du cho pa la
kon chog sum gyi jin lab jug par shog

Offering Food

Visualize the food as blissful wisdom nectar inside a vast jewelled vessel, and offer this to a small Buddha visualized at your heart chakra. Recite, "OM AH HUM" three times to consecrate the food and then offer it with any of the following verses:

Guru is Buddha, Guru is Dharma, Guru is Sangha also.
Guru is the originator of all (goodness and happiness).
To all Gurus, I make this offering.

You, whose body was formed by a million perfect virtues,
Whose speech fulfils the hopes of all beings,
Whose mind perceives all that is to be known,
To the prince of the Shakyas I make this offering.

The supreme teacher, the precious Buddha,
The supreme practice, the holy precious Dharma,
The supreme guide, the precious Sangha,
To all of the objects of refuge, I make this offering.

As you eat, imagine that Guru Shakyamuni Buddha at your heart experiences bliss from the nectar that you have offered to him. He radiates light which fills your entire body.

Dedicate the positive potential (merit) created by offering the food:

May we and those around us, in all future lives,
Never be separated from the Three Jewels,
Continuously make offerings to the Three Jewels,
And receive the inspiration of the Three Jewels.

When you dedicate, especially remember the sentient beings who created negative karma by harming others and who suffered and died in the process of growing and preparing the food.

The Eight Mahayana Precepts Ceremony

Introduction

The eight mahayana precepts are taken for twenty-four hours. It is especially good to take them on full and new moon days and on other Buddhist festival days. Observing precepts for even such a short time has tremendous benefits: one accumulates a great amount of positive potential (merit) in a short time. One will receive upper rebirths and eventually will attain enlightenment. One is protected from harm and the place where one lives becomes peaceful and prosperous. One's mind is peaceful and calm; one gains control over one's bad habits; there are fewer distractions when meditating. One gets along better with others. One will meet the Buddha's teachings in the future and can be born as a disciple of Maitreya Buddha.

The eight precepts are:

1. Avoid killing, directly or indirectly.
2. Avoid stealing and taking things without the permission of their owner.
3. Avoid sexual contact.
4. Avoid lying and deceiving others.
5. Avoid intoxicants: alcohol, tobacco and drugs (except for medicinal purposes).

6. Avoid eating more than one meal that day. The meal is taken before noon, and once one has stopped eating for thirty minutes, the meal is considered finished. At other times of the day one can take light drinks, but not undiluted whole milk or fruit juice with pulp. Avoid eating black foods: meat, eggs, onions, garlic and radishes.
7. Avoid sitting on a high, expensive bed or seat with pride. Also avoid sitting on animal skins.
8. Avoid wearing jewellery, perfume, and make-up. Avoid singing, dancing or playing music with attachment.

For a precept to be broken completely, four conditions must be present:

1. The motivation is a negative attitude such as attachment, anger, etc.
2. There is an object of the action, e.g. a being that is killed or an object that is stolen.
3. One does the action. If one tells someone else to kill, steal or lie, it is also a transgression.
4. The action is completed, e.g. the being dies before oneself or one thinks, "This is mine."

The first time one takes the precepts, it is done from a Master. Thereafter, one can do the ceremony before a Buddha image by regarding it as the actual Buddha.

Preliminary Prayers

First recite the morning prayers. Then sit down and recite the seven limb prayer, and the mandala offering. Generate a strong wish to attain enlightenment for the benefit of all sentient beings, and with that motivation, kneel down and take the precepts.

Taking the Precepts

chog chu na sug pay sang gye dang/ jang chub sem pa tam chay
dag la gong su sol

lo pon gong su sol (Omit if taking in front of a Buddha image.)
ji tar ngon gyi de zhin sheg pa, dra chom pa, yang dag par dzog
pay sang gye, ta chang shay ta wu/ lang po chen po/ ja wa jay
shing je pa jay pa/ kur bor wa/ rang gi don je su tob pa/ si par
kun tu jor wa yong su zay pa/ yang dag pay ka/ leg par nam
par drol way tug/ leg par nam par drol way shay rab chen de
dag gi/ sem chen tam che kyi don gyi chir dang/ pen par ja way
chir dang/ drol war ja way chir dang/ mu gay may par ja way
chir dang/ nay me par ja way chir dang/ jang chub kyi chog kyi
cho nam yong su dzog par ja way chir dang/ la na may pa yang
dag par dzog pay jang chub nge par tog par ja way chir so jong
yang dag par dzay pa de zhin du dag (say your name) zhe gyi
way kyang/ du di nay zung tay ji si sang nyi ma ma shar gyi
bar du/ sem chen tam che kyi don gyi chir dang/ pen par ja way
chir dang/ drol war ja way chir dang/ mu gay may par ja way
chir dang/ nay may par ja way chir dang/ jang chub kyi chog
kyi cho nam yong su dzog par ja way chir dang/ la na may pa
yang dag par dzog pay jang chug nge par tog par ja way chir
so jong yang dag par lang war gyi wo   3x

Taking the Precepts

All Buddhas and bodhisattvas residing in the ten directions, please pay attention to me!
Preceptor, please pay attention to me! (Omit if taking before a Buddha image.)

Just as the past tathagatas, the foe destroyers and the completely perfect Buddhas, like the heavenly steed and the great elephant, accomplished their objective and did their task, laid down their load (of the contaminated aggregates), achieved their own purpose, comsumed their ties to samsara; as they possessed perfect speech, a mind properly liberated, a wisdom properly liberated; just as they perfectly took the mahayana precepts for the sake of all sentient beings, in order to benefit them, in order to liberate them, in order to eliminate famine, in order to eliminate sickness, in order to perfect the thirty-seven aids to enlightenment, and in order to realize the highest perfect enlightenment; in the same way, for the sake of all sentient beings, in order to benefit them, in order to liberate them, in order to eliminate famine, in order to eliminate sickness, in order to perfect the thirty-seven aids to enlightenment, and in order to realize the highest perfect enlightenment, I, (say your name), will also perfectly accept the mahayana precepts from this moment until sunrise tomorrow.   3x

Prayer of Commitment to Keep the Precepts

deng nay sog cho mi ja zhing
zhen gyi nor yang lang mi ja
trig pay chog kyang mi cho ching
dzun gyi tsig kyang mi ma o
kyon ni mang po nyer ten pay
chang ni yong su pang war ja
tri ten che to mi ja zhing
de zhin du ma yin pay zay
dri dang treng wa gyen dang ni
gar dang lu sog pang war ja
ji tar dra chom tag tu ni
sog cho la sog mi je tar
de zhin sog cho la sog pang
la may jang chub nyur tob shog
dug ngel mang trug jig ten di
si pay tso lay drol war shog

Dharani of Pure Morality

om ahmoga shila sambara bara bara maha shuda sato
payma bibu kita budza dara dara samanta ahwalokite hum
pay soha.

Dedication Prayers

trim kyi tsul trim kyon me ching
tsul trim nam par dag dang den
lom sen may pay tsul trim kyi
tsul trim pa rol chin dzog shog

Follow this by other dedication prayers.

Prayer of Commitment to Keep the Precepts

From now on I will not kill, or take another's property. I will not engage in sexual activity and will not speak false words. I will totally avoid alcohol, which is the cause of many faults. I will not use high or expensive beds or thrones. I will avoid eating food at improper times. I will not wear perfumes, garlands and ornaments, or sing, dance and so forth. Just as the foe destroyers abandoned killing and so forth, may I, by avoiding killing and so forth, quickly attain the highest enlightenment. May I be freed from the ocean of cyclic existence, this world disturbed by many sorrows.

Dharani of Pure Morality

om ahmoga shila sambara bara bara maha shuda sato payma bibu kita budza dara dara samanta ahwalokite hum pey soha   21x

Dedication Prayers

By having the flawless morality of the Dharma law, pure morality, and morality without conceit, may I complete the perfection of morality.

Follow this by reciting other dedication prayers.

Practicing Dharma in Daily Life
by Venerable Zopa Rinpoche

When Zopa Rinpoche stayed in Singapore in May, 1988, he stayed at the home of a happy and very devoted family. Before leaving, Rinpoche, with his great compassion dictated the following to me to compile for the Lim family, especially the mother, to practice. He suggested it also be included in this book, so that others could learn how to transform daily life activities into the path to enlightenment.

Waking Up

In the morning when you wake up, visualize the Buddha on the crown of your head and think, "How fortunate I am that so far I have not died. Again today I have the opportunity to practice the Dharma. I again have the opportunity to take the essence of this human rebirth which has so many freedoms and richnesses. The great essence to be taken from this opportunity is to practice bodhicitta, the mind that is dedicated to attaining enlightenment for the benefit of all sentient beings, by renouncing myself and cherishing others. Cherishing only myself is the greatest obstacle to being happy myself and it is especially the greatest hindrance to bringing about the happiness of all sentient beings. So, from now on, I will never allow myself to be under the control of the self-cherishing thought.

"Also, cherishing others is the best means to bring all success for my own happiness and especially to successfully bring about the happiness that all sentient beings desire. Therefore, from now on, I will never separate from the precious bodhicitta, the mind cherishing other sentient beings, for even one moment. With the bodhicitta, and the mind that cherishes others, I will live my life."

Then make a sincere request to the Buddha, "Whether my life is happy or painful, may whatever actions I do with my body, speech and mind always become *only* the cause to lead quickly the pitiful mother sentient beings throughout infinite space to enlightenment."

Guru Shakyamuni Buddha is extremely pleased with your request. He melts into light, which flows down through your crown to your heart, blessing, inspiring and transforming your mind. Think, "I have received all of the Buddha's qualities." Then imagine a small Buddha made of light appears at your heart. Throughout the day, think of the Buddha constantly. In this way, you will become more mindful of what you do, say and think, as you will be aware of Buddha witnessing it.

Read and contemplate the "Eight Verses of Thought Transformation":

1. With the thought of attaining enlightenment
   For the welfare of all beings,
   Who are more precious than a wish-fulfilling jewel,
   I will constantly practice holding them dear.

2. Whenever I am with others
   I will practice seeing myself as the lowest of all,
   And from the very depths of my heart
   I will respectfully hold others as supreme.

3. In all actions I will examine my mind
   And the moment a disturbing attitude arises,
   Endangering myself and others,
   I will firmly confront and avert it.

4. Whenever I meet a person of bad nature
   Who is overwhelmed by negative energy and intense suffering,
   I will hold such a rare one dear, As if I had found a precious
   treasure.

5. When others, out of jealousy,
   Mistreat me with abuse, slander and so on,
   I will practice accepting defeat And offering the victory to them.

6. When someone I have benefited
   And in whom I have placed great trust
   Hurts me very badly,
   I will practice seeing that person as my supreme teacher.

7. In short, I will offer directly and indirectly
   Every benefit and happiness to all beings, my mothers.
   I will practice in secret taking upon myself
   All their harmful actions and sufferings.

8. Without these practices being defiled by the stains of the eight
   worldly concerns
   And by perceiving all phenomena as illusory,
   I will practice without grasping to release all beings
   From the bondage of the disturbing unsubdued mind and
   karma.

By remembering Guru Shakyamuni Buddha, do your daily life
actions as follows:

Eating and Drinking

Before you eat or drink, think, "I am going to make this food (drink) offering to Guru Shakyamuni Buddha, who is the embodiment of·all the Buddhas, Dharma, and Sangha, in order to achieve enlightenment for the sake of all mother sentient beings." Think the food is very pure and sweet nectar that gives great bliss. Its taste is delicious, like what the Buddha experiences; that is, it is completely beyond the usual ordinary appearance of food. Offer the food with the prayers contained in this book, and imagine the Buddha at your heart experiencing bliss as you eat.

Enjoying Sense Objects

Whatever sense objects you enjoy during the day — cloths, music, beautiful scenery and so forth — think that you are offering them to Guru Shakyamuni Buddha who is at your heart. In this way, you continuously make offerings to the Buddha, thus creating a great store of positive potential. Also, you will become less attached to sense pleasures and will begin to enjoy them with a peaceful mind.

Making Offerings on the Altar

Think, "I am going to make these offerings in order to achieve enightenment for the benefit of all pitiful mother sentient beings who have been kind to me since beginningless rebirths." Immediately consecrate whatever you offer by saying, "OM AH HUM."

When you look at the pictures and statues of the Buddhas and holy beings on your altar, think that they are all the Guru and the Buddhas, Dharma and Sangha of the ten directions. Offer to them with this recognition, and imagine that they generate great bliss by receiving your offerings. Think that you are offering to the Buddhas, bodhisattvas, arhats and sanghas of the ten directions. Offer to the statues of the Buddhas and deities (which represent Buddha's holy body), to all the scriptures (which represent the Buddha's holy speech), and to all the stupas (which represent the Buddha's holy mind) that exist in all ten directions. This includes making offerings to all holy objects in Tibet, in India and in each person's home where there is a holy object. This is the most skilful way to accumulate merit. In this way, you make offerings to each and every holy object without needing to take even one step or spend even one dollar to travel to those places. By thinking that all the statues, Buddhas, bodhisattvas and so forth are manifestations of the Guru, you accumulate the highest merit.

After offering, think, "Whatever happiness and virtue I have accumulated, may all sentient beings receive it, and whatever suffering sentient beings have, may it ripen upon me." Then dedicate the positive potential.

Working

When you go to work, think, "I must achieve enlightenment in order to lead each and every sentient being to enlightenment. Therefore, I am going to do service for sentient beings by going to work." If you are working in order to provide for your family, it is service to sentient beings. If you do not have to provide for your family, you nevertheless need the necessary material conditions in order to practice the Dharma so that you may attain enlightenment for the benefit of all sentient beings.

While you are at work, remember the kindness of the other sentient beings who gave you the job and who make it possible for you to earn a living. Thinking in this way helps to avoid generating negative emotions like anger at work.

Bathing

Think, "I am going bathe by transforming this action into the cause to attain enlightenment for the benefit of all sentient beings." By thinking in a new way, you can make your shower or bath a purification practice. One way to think is that the water is very blissful and you are offering it to the Buddha at your heart. Another way is to visualize whichever manifestation of the Buddha you feel a strong connection with (for example, Chenresig or Tara) above your head and think that the bathing water is flowing from his/her hand. The water is the nature of wisdom and it is making your mind clear so you can practice the path for the benefit of sentient beings. While you are washing, think that all negative karmas, sicknesses, and interfering forces are cleansed by the wisdom realizing emptiness and that you receive all the realizations and qualities of the Buddha.

Sleeping

At the end of the day it is important to purify the negative actions created during the day. The most powerful method to do this is by means of the four opponent powers:

1. Taking refuge and generating bodhicitta.
2. Having regret for the negative actions you have done.
3. Doing remedial actions, i.e. a purification practice.
4. Determining not to do the action again in the future.

By doing this, it stops the karma from multiplying each day, each week, each month. It also purifies the negative karma accumulated since beginningless time. By thus cleansing your obstacles, you have the opportunity to become enlightened.

Before going to bed, think, "I take refuge in the Buddha, Dharma and Sangha until I am enlightened. By practicing generosity and the other far-reaching attitudes, may I attain Buddhahood for the benefit of the migrating beings."

Visualize Guru Vajrasattva on your crown. Light and nectar flow down from his heart into you and purify all negative karmas and obscurations of yourself and others. While visualizing in this way, recite Vajrasattva's mantra at least twenty-eight times:

Om vajrasattva hum.

Then Vajrasattva says to you, "All of your negative karmas and obscurations are completely purified. Be happy about this." Vajrasattva absorbs to your heart and blesses your mind.

Dedicate the positive potential:

May the precious bodhi mind
Not yet born arisé and grow.
May that born have no decline,
But increase forever more.

In all my lives, with the Victorious One, Lama Tzong Khapa, acting in person as the Mahayana Guru, may I never turn aside for even an instant from the excellent path praised by the Victorious Ones.

Due to the positive potentials accumulated by myself and others in the past, present and future, may anyone who merely sees, hears, remembers, touches or talks to me be freed in that very instant from all sufferings and abide in happiness forever.

When you go to bed, think, "I am going to practice sleeping yoga in order to achieve enlightenment for the benefit of all sentient beings." Lie down in the lion position, which is how Buddha lay when he passed away: lie on your right side, with your right hand under your cheek. Your left hand is on your left thigh, and your legs are extended. Remember the kindness and sufferings of sentient beings and go to sleep feeling loving-kindness towards them. Visualize Guru Shakyamuni Buddha on your pillow, and put your head in his lap. Very gentle light flows from the Buddha into you, and by remembering the Buddha's enlightened qualities with devotion, fall asleep.

The Six Preparatory Practices

Prior to the first meditation session of the day, it is good to do the six preparatory practices:

1. Sweep and clean the room and arrange the altar.

2. Make offerings on the altar, e.g. light, food, incense, water bowls, etc.

3. Sit in a comfortable position and examine your mind. If there is much distraction, do some breathing meditation to calm your mind. Then establish a good motivation. After that, take refuge and generate the dedicated heart by reciting the appropriate prayers.

4. Visualize the merit field with the Gurus, Buddhas, bodhisattvas, etc. If this is too difficult, visualize Shakyamuni Buddha alone and consider him the embodiment of all Buddhas, Dharma and Sangha.

5. Offer the seven limb prayer and the mandala, by reciting those prayers.

6. Make requests to the lineage Gurus for inspiration by reciting the requesting prayers.

It is also good to review the entire graduated path to enlightenment by reciting for example, "Foundation of All Excellence." This helps you to understand the purpose of the particular meditation that you will do in the overall scheme of training the mind in the gradual path. It also plants the seed for you to obtain each realization of the path. Then, do analytical meditation, thinking about one of the topics below by remembering and applying the explanations you have heard or read on the subject.

Meditations of the Gradual Path to Enlightenment

1. Relying whole-heartedly on a Spiritual Master (Guru)
   a. Advantages of properly relying and disadvantageous of not properly relying on a Spiritual Master
   b. How to rely by one's thought
   c. How to rely by one's actions

2. Precious human rebirth
   a. 8 freedoms and 10 endowments of a precious human rebirth
   b. Its great value
   c. Its rarity

Path of the lower being — striving for the happiness of future lives

3. Recollecting death
   a. Death is certain to occur
   b. The time of death is uncertain
   c. Nothing except the Dharma helps at the time of death

4. Considering the sufferings of the lower realms
   a. Hell realm
   b. Hungry ghost realm
   c. Animal realm

5. Taking refuge, a safe and sound direction in life
   a. Causes for refuge: dread, faith, compassion
   b. Objects of refuge: Buddha, Dharma, Sangha
   c. How to take refuge: knowing the qualities etc. of the Three Jewels
   d. Advantages of taking refuge
   e. What to practice after taking refuge

6. Generating confidence in the functioning of cause and effect
   a. General aspects of cause and effect
      1. Karma is definite: positive actions bring happiness, negative ones bring pain.
      2. The weight of karma increases as time passes.
      3. If the cause is not created, the effect is not experienced.
      4. Karmic imprints are not lost, but will ripen when conditions become favorable.
   b. Specific aspects
      1. Cause and effect of negative, destructive actions
      2. Factors making an action heavy or light
      3. Cause and effect of positive, constructive actions
      4. Four results that a complete action can bring
      5. Causes of the 8 favorable qualities for Dharma practice

Path of the intermediate being — striving for liberation from cyclic existence (Contemplating the Four Noble Truths)

7. Sufferings of cyclic existence
   a. General sufferings of samsara
      1. Six sufferings: uncertainty, dissatisfaction, having to die, having to be reborn, going up and down in the six realms, experiencing pain by oneself alone.
      2. Three sufferings: pain, change, pervading-compounded
   b. Sufferings of the three upper realms
      1. Human: birth, sickness, aging, death, parted from what you like, meeting what you do not like, not getting what you want, having contaminated aggregates
      2. Demi-god: jealousy and quarrels
      3. God: great suffering prior to death

8. Functioning of cyclic existence and the path to liberation
   a. Causes of suffering: how ignorance causes the other delusions which in turn produces karma that propels us from one rebirth to the next. 12 links of dependent arising.

   b. Path to liberation: the three higher trainings of morality, concentration and wisdom

Path of the superior being — striving for enlightenment for the benefit of all sentient beings

9. Advantages of the dedicated heart which wants to attain enlightenment for the benefit of all sentient beings (bodhicitta)

10. The way to develop the dedicated heart
   a. Seven points of cause and effect
      1. Equanimity between friend, enemy and stranger is the preliminary
      2. Seven points: recognizing sentient beings as your mother, remembering their kindness, wishing to repay it, heart-warming love, compassion, great determination, dedicated heart
   b. Equalizing and exchanging self and others: equalizing self and others, disadvantages of selfishness, advantages of cherishing others, exchanging self and others, taking others' suffering and giving them your happiness and its causes
   c. Combining the above two methods into one

11. Taking the bodhisattva vows
   a. Aspiring dedicated heart
   b. Engaging dedicated heart — 18 root and 46 auxillary vows

12. Conduct of a bodhisattva
   a. Six far-reaching attitudes (perfections) — generosity, morality, patience, joyous effort, concentration, wisdom
   b. How to develop concentration and wisdom in particular
   c. Special path of the Vajrayana

Guidelines for the Practice of Refuge

Having taken refuge, a safe and sound direction, in the Three Jewels — Buddha, Dharma, and Sangha — it is advantageous to follow certain guidelines for practice in order to make progress along the path to enlightenment.

++ In analogy to taking refuge in the Buddha, commit yourself whole-heartedly to a qualified spiritual master.

++ In analogy to taking refuge in the Dharma, listen to and study the teachings as well as put them into practice in your daily life.

++ In analogy to taking refuge in the Sangha, respect the Sangha as your spiritual companions and follow the good examples they set.

++ Avoid being rough and arrogant, running after any desirable object you see and criticizing anything that meets with your disapproval. Be friendly and kind to others and be concerned more with correcting your own faults than with pointing out those of others.

++ As much as possible avoid the ten non-virtuous actions, and take and keep precepts.[22]

++ Have a compassionate and sympathetic heart towards all other sentient beings.

++ Make special offerings to the Three Jewels on Buddhist festival days.

Guidelines in Terms of Each of the Three Jewels

1. Having taken refuge in the Buddha, who has purified all defilements and develop all qualities, do not turn for refuge in worldly deities, who lack the capacity to guide you from all problems.

   Respect all images of the Buddha: do not put them in low or dirty places, step over them, point your feet towards them, sell them to earn a living or use them as collateral. When looking at various images, do not discriminate, "This Buddha is beautiful, but this one is not." Do not treat with respect expensive and impressive statues while neglecting those that are damaged or less costly.

2. Having taken refuge in the Dharma, avoid harming any living being.

   Also, respect the written words which describe the path to enlightenment by keeping the texts clean and in a high place. Avoid stepping over them, putting them on the floor, or throwing them in the rubbish when they are old. It is best to burn old Dharma materials.

3. Having taken refuge in the Sangha, do not cultivate the friendship of people who criticize the Buddha, Dharma, and Sangha or who have unruly behavior or do many harmful actions. By becoming friendly with such people, you can be influenced in the wrong way by them. However, that does not mean you should criticize or not have compassion for them.

Also, respect monks and nuns as they are people who are making earnest efforts to actualize the teachings. Respecting them helps your mind, for you appreciate their qualities and are open to learn from their example. By respecting even the robes of ordained beings, you will be happy and inspired when seeing them.

Common Guidelines

1. Mindful of the qualities, skills, and differences between the Three Jewels and other possible refuges, repeatedly take refuge in the Buddha, Dharma and Sangha.

2. Remembering their kindness, make offerings to them, especially offering your food before eating. (See the prayers for this.)

3. Mindful of their compassion, encourage others to take refuge in the Three Jewels.

4. Remembering the benefits of taking refuge, do so three times in the morning and three times in the evening, by reciting and reflecting upon any of the refuge prayers.

5. Do all actions by entrusting yourself to the Three Jewels.

6. Do not forsake your refuge at the cost of our life, or even as a joke.

A Note on the Translation

In preparing this book, sometimes a number of translations of the same prayers were consulted and integrated. Thubten Dekyong then checked them. Choosing an appropriate English word for many Tibetan terms was difficult, and each person will have his/her own preference. Below are alternative translations of a few terms. If one appeals to you more than another, feel free to substitute it when you say the prayers.

— Guru = Spiritual Master
— bodhicitta, bodhi mind = dedicated heart (or the heart dedicated to attaining enlightenment for the benefit of all sentient beings)
— determination to be free = renunciation
— bless = inspire [23]
— six far-reaching attitudes = six perfections
— Victorious Ones, Conquerors = the Buddhas
— spiritual children = bodhisattvas
— positive potential = merit
— migrating beings = beings born within cyclic existence. They migrate from one body to another under the influence of disturbing emotions and karma.
— karma = actions of our body, speech and mind

An effort was also made to simplify the phonetics, although that meant sacrificing some of the accuracy.

Notes

1. There are three objects of refuge: the Buddha, Dharma and Sangha. The Guru is not a fourth refuge. Guru refers to the blissful omniscient minds of all the Buddhas, and thus encompasses all three refuges. The blissful omniscient mind, which is purified of all obscurations and has developed its good qualities completely, is the Buddha. By being the true path and true cessation, it is the Dharma. By directly realizing emptiness, it is the Sangha.

2. The vows of individual liberation include the five lay precepts, the vows of novice and fully-ordained monks and nuns, and the one-day vows.

3. The three moral practices are restraining from negative actions, accumulating virtuous ones, and working for the benefit of sentient beings.

4. Objects are false in that their way of appearance and way of existence do not accord, i.e. although objects appear to be inherently existent, in fact they are not; they are empty of inherent existence.

5. Calm abiding is samatha, and special insight is vipassana.

6. The common path is the general path of the sutrayana (determination to be free, dedicated heart, wisdom realizing emptiness) and the path of the three lower tantras.

7. Vajrayana (the tantric path) is a branch of the Mahayana and contains special techniques for transforming one's ordinary body, speech and mind into the body, speech and mind of a Buddha.

8. The two stages are the generation stage and the completion stage of the highest class of tantra.

9. Vajradhara is the form that Shakyamuni Buddha appeared in when he taught the tantras.

10. The snow lions are manifestations of bodhisattvas, and their function is to dispel all obstacles and interferences. This means that their realizations dispel all internal obstacles — the disturbing attitudes and contaminated karmas (actions) which are the source of all of our problems. The Buddha's seat represents the three principal realizations of the path: the lotus symbolizes the determination to be free from cyclic existence; the moon represents the heart dedicated to attaining enlightenment for the benefit of all sentient beings; the sun is the wisdom realizing emptiness.

11. The blissful wisdom nectar cures the four maras: 1) the disturbing attitudes of attachment, anger, ignorance, etc.; 2) our contaminated aggregates of body and mind; 3) uncontrolled death; 4) worldly gods who can interfere with our practice.

12. See Maitreya's *Abhisamayalamkara* for a detailed description of the features of the Buddha's body.

13. The qualities of the Buddha's body include his ability to transform his body into different forms, animate and inanimate, in order to help sentient beings according to their individual needs and inclinations. With his speech, he can communicate different aspects of the Dharma simultaneously to beings of various levels of development and can be understood by them in their respective languages. His omniscient mind of wisdom and compassion clearly sees everything that exists and knows the thoughts and experiences of every sentient being.

14. If you have received a full initiation which enables you to visualize yourself as the deity, then instead of visualizing a small Buddha at your heart, you may visualize yourself as the Buddha.

15. The Buddhas are called the Ones Thus Gone (Sanskrit: Tatagata) because they have gone beyond the misery of cyclic existence to complete enlightenment and thus have abandoned all defilements and subtle obscurations. They also have realized the ultimate nature of all phenomena, thusness or emptiness.

16. The five heinous actions are: causing a schism in the Sangha, killing one's father, killing one's mother, killing an arhat, and drawing blood from the Buddha's body.

17. The ten non-virtuous actions are: killing, stealing, sexual misconduct, (three of the body); lying, divisive speech, harsh words, idle talk, (four of speech); covetous thinking, maliciousness, and wrong views (three of mind).

18. The five close-to-heinous actions are: killing a bodhisattva, killing a superior being (one who has realized emptiness directly), stealing the provisions or funds of the Sangha community, destroying a monastery or stupa with anger, commiting incest with one's mother who is an arhat.

19. The vows of individual liberation include the five lay precepts as well as the precepts of the novice and fully-ordained monk and nun, and the one-day vows.

20. The trainings of the bodhisattva include the guidelines for aspiring bodhicitta and the 18 root and 46 auxillary bodhisattva precepts.

21. The tantric commitments include the 14 root and 8 auxillary tantric vows, the 19 samaya of the five Buddha families, and other commitments taken at the time of empowerment into practices of the highest class of tantra.

22. For a lay person, one can take the eight Mahayana precepts for one day, or one can take some or all of the five precepts for the duration of one's life. On the basis of refuge, a lay person may also take bodhisattva precepts and tantric vows.

23. The term "inspire" or "bless" means to transform our mind. A blessing is not like an object given from Master to student. A student has received "blessing" or has been inspired when his/her own mind transforms into the Dharma, i.e. when the student has understood and integrated the meaning of the teachings into his/her life.

Sponsors

The printing of this book was made possible through the kind
generosity of the following people:

an anonymous sponsor
Ang Chwee Hwee and family
Mok family

Lee Siew Cheung
Tina Leong
Robert Gwee
Kathy Leong

The late Jimmy Quat
Yeong Khoong
Tan Yong Kwang
Bryan Quah
Hua Zhen

Tan Boon Hwee and family
Tan Poh Beng and family
Yap Kim Fong

Lim Boon Eng
Ven. Meng Liang
Elsie Ng

Lim Lay Guat
Tan Poh Geok
Lee Yong Seng
Teo Siew Khim

Ong Choon Lim
Ho Siew Khim
Lim Choi Sin
Lim Eng Tiong
Ng Ah Bak
Lee Mei Yi
Lee Junquiao
Ong Eng Keang
Ruby Cheah,
in memory of her father

Roland Kubler
Rosalind
Ann Kuek
Alice Chua
and other benefactors